UNDERSTA
Your 6 year old

UNDERSTANDING
Your 6 year old

Deborah Steiner

of the

TAVISTOCK CLINIC

Series Editor: Elsie Osborne

ROSENDALE PRESS

Copyright © 1993 The Tavistock Clinic

First published in Great Britain in 1993 by:
Rosendale Press Ltd
Premier House, 10 Greycoat Place
London SW1P 1SB

All rights reserved. No part of this publication
may be reproduced, stored in a retrieval system
or transmitted, in any form or by any means
electronic, mechanised, photocopying,
recording, or otherwise, without the prior
permission of the copyright owner.

Design by Pep Reiff
Production Edward Allhusen
Typeset by Ace Filmsetting Ltd
Printed in the United Kingdom by Redwood Press

British Library Cataloguing in Publication Data
A catalogue record for this book is available from
The British Library

ISBN 1 872803 35 0

The Tavistock Clinic, London, was founded in 1920, in order to meet the needs of people whose lives had been disrupted by the First World War. Today, it is still committed to understanding people's needs though, of course, times and people have changed. Now, as well as working with adults and adolescents, the Tavistock Clinic has a large department for children and families. This offers help to parents who are finding the challenging task of bringing up their children daunting and has, therefore, a wide experience of children of all ages. It is firmly committed to early intervention in the inevitable problems that arise as children grow up, and to the view that if difficulties are caught early enough, parents are the best people to help their children with them. Professional Staff of the Clinic were, therefore, pleased to be able to contribute to this series of books to describe the ordinary development of children, to help in spotting the growing pains and to provide ways that parents might think about their children's growth.

THE AUTHOR

After completing a language degree at London University, **Deborah Steiner** worked part-time as a primary school teacher and wrote for BBC Radio Schools and ITV Childrens Television. She trained as a Child Psychotherapist at the Tavistock Clinic and now works as a Senior Child Psychotherapist at Enfield Child and Family Service. She is on the visiting staff of the Tavistock Clinic. She trained as a psychoanalyst at the Institute of Psychoanalysis and works in private practice as an analyst. She is married with three children.

Publications include "The Internal Family and The Facts of Life" *Journal of Psycho-analytic Psychotherapy* (1989) Vol 4 No 1.

ACKNOWLEDGEMENTS

I would like to thank Mrs Priscilla Roth for her helpful comments and suggestions when I was writing this book.

The poem "Now we are Six" from *Now we are Six* by A. A. Milne is reproduced with permission from Methuen Childrens Books.

CONTENTS

                                                                                  Page

INTRODUCTION   11
"Now we are Six"

CHAPTER 1 THINKING AND LEARNING   15
The nature of intelligence – rivalry and competitiveness – learning to read – dyslexia – maths – how can parents help?

CHAPTER 2 NEW RELATIONSHIPS   34
Adjustments – the teacher – schoolfriends

**CHAPTER 3 THE SIX YEAR OLD AND
THE FACTS OF LIFE**   48
Old age – talking about death – illness – sexuality and birth – dangers – child abuse – where does God live? – fantasy and fairy stories

**CHAPTER 4 THE SIX YEAR OLD AND
EVERYDAY LIFE**   64
Coming home – separation and divorce – bringing things home – television and computer games – discipline

FURTHER READING   78

HELPFUL ORGANISATIONS   79

INTRODUCTION

When I was One
I had just begun

When I was Two
I was nearly new

When I was Three
I was hardly me.

When I was Four
I was not much more.

When I was Five
I was just alive.

But now I am Six, I'm as clever as clever.
So I think I'll be six now for ever and ever.

A.A. Milne

The final poem in A. A. Milne's book *Now we are Six*, captures with a few deft strokes the sense of the important changes that have already taken place in a child's life. Your six year old, now in the second year of infant school, is leaving infancy behind and embarking on childhood. If all has gone well, the teething troubles of starting school will have largely been resolved and the child can concentrate on the task of finding a place in the world, and developing new intellectual skills. The new status of no longer being the youngest in the school sometimes helps to make the second year child feel more confident, proud and perhaps a little superior to the children just beginning school.

By this stage children's capacity to think in an abstract way is much increased and they can imagine things now in a way that was not possible at an earlier stage. For example they can not only count up to 10 but they can also have a concept of a group of 10 – and they can begin to understand that 10 objects do not change in number even if you cover them up or move them around. This seems so elementary to adults that it is easy to underestimate the effort and perseverance the child needs to make to achieve this step forward. What our six year old lacks now is experience and the work and activities at school will provide much of that experience. At this stage most children are eager to learn the "whys and wherefores" of the physical world and this quality of exuberant curiosity makes them fun to be with and a pleasure to teach.

The period from now until about twelve is sometimes referred to as "latency". The notion behind this term is that our toddlers' preoccupations with bodily feelings and func-

INTRODUCTION

tions, particularly their own and their parents', begin to subside and to be replaced by a spurt in intellectual activity. The sense of separateness which was already beginning at the end of the first year is more firmly established; latency children are now turning their attention to finding out about the wider world and what kind of a place they can have in it.

Children of six are already capable to some extent of controlling intense feelings and channelling them into more orderly and thoughtful explorations so that they can use their minds to find out about the world around them. In this book we will be considering the various ways six year olds carry their early learning experiences into the outside world, and build on them to discover more about their own strengths and limitations.

We have seen throughout the previous books in this series how children gradually begin to be interested and involved in the world outside themselves, beginning with mother, the parents as a couple, then the family and now, beyond. They are also interested in feelings and relationships – what makes other people "tick" and what makes other people different from themselves and from their own family. Feelings such as love and hate, friendship, rivalry, competitiveness, and jealousy continue to play a vital role in the child's social and intellectual life.

Many parents reading this book will be very aware of the endless questions children of this age pose about how things work and why certain things happen. Their questions can often be startling and sometimes discomfiting in their directness and some of these will be discussed later in the book.

There is now a marked shift as the child's centre of interest moves more and more away from home and into school life. Relationships at school, with classmates and the teachers, become extremely important, and the vicissitudes of these relationships may be a source of great enrichment in the childs mental life as well as a cause of distress and anxiety at the times when they go wrong. However settled your six year old is, the excitement of new things to learn together with the pressures to get along with classmates, and probably a new teacher, will add up to a strenuous and tiring day.

At the same time this is an exciting and liberating period in a child's life and part of the difficult task for parents is to give encouragement and support, while having to tolerate an increasing awareness of interests and experiences which their child is now learning to manage alone, and from which they are inevitably excluded. One purpose of this book will be to discuss some of these issues and the dilemmas that face parents in their everyday life with their six year old.

It seems important to say right at the beginning that much of what is said of a six year old may also apply to some five year olds or some seven year olds, as children develop at vastly different speeds and in diverse ways according to their interests and aptitudes.

CHAPTER ONE

THINKING AND LEARNING

Once the six year old is established in school, the parents' focus of concern will become their child's progress in learning to read and write and do maths. They are understandably concerned that he or she gets off to a good educational start, and it is well recognised that skilful and sympathetic teaching at this stage is crucial if children are to achieve what they are capable of. But it is also important to recognise that childrens' abilities and aptitudes vary enormously both in degree and diversity. In fact it may not be evident yet what your child's particular strengths and weaknesses are. Of course parents get anxious when their child seems to be slow or lagging behind but it often turns out that a child who seems like this in the infant school then puts on a spurt in the junior school, or even later and its worth bearing this in mind before jumping to the conclusion that your child is lacking in intelligence.

The nature of intelligence

The issue of intelligence is a complex and thorny one as so many factors play a part in the speed and direction in which a child develops intellectually. To a certain degree intelligence is hereditary and over this parents, perhaps luckily, have no control. However it is also widely recognised that emotional factors and experiences from very early infancy play a significant role in the child's capacity to develop intelligence by learning. Within the same family it may be that by the age of six one child seems to be brighter or quicker than an older one was at the same age. It is tempting sometimes to assume that an active, outgoing or talkative child is bound to be more intelligent than a child with a quieter or more retiring temperament; in fact the opposite may be true.

However there may be real differences in ability and aptitudes which have to be recognised and come to terms with, both by the parents and the children as such a state of affairs will undoubtedly present difficulties. One mother reported that her daughter Zoë, nearly seven, had begun to ask her parents persistently if they loved her which made them feel guilty and worried. Zoë had an older sister who had recently got a place at a sought after school in the area and her parents were naturally delighted and pleased with her. This was a family in which much emphasis was put on academic achievement and it seemed as though Zoë was experiencing some anxiety about whether her parents would continue to love her if she was not so successful. It was also helpful for Zoë's parents to be aware that her anxiety seemed to escalate as her own impending move to junior school drew nearer. It

THINKING AND LEARNING

is a very difficult task for a younger child who has an older brother or sister doing more grown up things, to maintain a confident wish to learn while having to bear not being able to do the kind of school work that the older ones are doing. It is also a sensitive issue for parents to deal with, in their struggle to provide the right level of encouragement for children at different stages.

In the seventh year of life many intellectual skills become available to children as they mature and gain experience of the world around them. For example, a five year old boy was shown two equal-sized balls of plasticine. He agreed that they were the same size. Then one of the balls was rolled out into a sausage-shaped piece. He was asked which lump contained the most plasticine. He now said that there was more plasticine in the sausage-shaped piece "because it was longer". By the time he was six and a half he could recognise that there was the same amount of plasticine in each lump even though they were of different shapes. The same kind of experiment can be done with two identical containers filled with the same amount of water. If the water from one container is put into a long thin vessel, a five year old would be likely to think the amounts of water would now be different, but a six or seven year old would be able to recognise that the amount of liquid does not just change because the shape of the container changes. To adults it seems very obvious that a ball of plasticine or a glass of water does not change in quantity when the shape or container is changed. To six year olds it is not readily obvious but they can begin to work out by thinking that although the plasticine may look bigger it is in reality the same. Such a major step forward does not take place quickly but over months, even years and a six year old child is on the threshhold of an exhilarating and exciting new view of the world. It is important for parents to have some understanding of the real differences in the way their six year old sees the world so that their expectations will be realistic and not overburdensome to the child. A parent who gets overly exasperated or anxious when their child is struggling may be expressing his or her own feelings of rivalry or need to have a clever child.

A child who is given the feeling of being dismissed as stupid whenever a mistake is made or whenever there is a difficulty in understanding something, will become less and less inclined to risk having a shot at new tasks and problems or persevering with them. The six year old making further bids for independence is still intensely bound up with the parents and acutely sensitive to their reactions to any forays into the outside world and attempts to learn. An experience at this stage of parents who are patient and encouraging when knowledge and understanding seem precarious, will remain with, and strengthen, a child's own capacity to be patient and persevering later on in life.

Rivalry and Competitiveness

Many parents feel anxious and upset when their small children are jealous and rivalrous with each other, especially when these feelings are very intense and powerful. It is as though any sign of such feelings means that they have failed as parents and would therefore reflect badly on them. This may stem from an unrealistic expectation that really good parents would be able, by scrupulously fair behaviour, to eliminate such troublesome emotions. In reality we know as adults how very much these kinds of feelings are a part of our every day life in relation to family, friends, and colleagues. We also know that such feelings can be disturbing and that we somehow have to find a way of managing and controlling them. More loving and friendly feelings come to our aid in this struggle although most people would acknowledge that they are more successful at some times than at others, often without quite knowing why. We also often try in all sorts of ways to avoid these painful feelings.

All this is true for our inexperienced six year old facing the new demands of school. We have seen in the earlier books in this series how these feelings exist even in the very early months, when the infant shows signs of jealousy and rivalry when parents are paying attention to each other, or to another child. These feelings and the ways that have been developed so far in managing them in the family, will go with the child into the classroom, although in a less raw and intense state, and will play an important role in the business of learning from the teacher and taking part in class activities.

There is a measure of aggression in being competitive – wanting to be the best, the fastest, the cleverest, the favourite or whatever, over and above others. Being competitive is also about wanting to gain and maintain a valued place in the world, at first in the world of home and family and now in the world of school. A child of six or seven will naturally have feelings of superiority and even triumph over a younger brother or sister. Lisa had just had her sixth birthday and like the child in the poem at the beginning, was very pleased with being six. She had had a new jigsaw puzzle given to her and was well on the way to completing it. Her three-year-old sister Anna was trying determinedly but quite unsuccessfully to put some of the pieces in prompting Lisa to get up with a rather theatrical sigh of exasperation and get Anna's block puzzle saying "here's your puzzle, silly. Look, its got little knobs to help you". Whether your child is able to use greater experience to some extent to help a younger one as Lisa was – albeit with more than a hint of scorn – or whether it is used as a means of making the younger one feel stupid or inferior is of great importance for both of them. A six year old who has been allowed to walk over the feelings of a younger brother or sister, or of a parent for that matter, is likely to find it much more difficult to compete in an ordinary, healthy way with classmates and friends at school, because competitiveness and therefore achievement is felt inwardly to be destructive and mean.

A sense of competitiveness can be a healthy asset, as it provides a spur to do well. For six year olds the need to be loved and valued by the parents on whom they still depend for emotional and physical well-being, continues to be very strong, particularly now in establishing a separate identity in the world outside. The degree of competitive drive in a child's personality may be to some extent innate, but the child's ability to master and use such feelings constructively in the process of learning will be determined in part by the experience of parents helping in the early years with the feelings of frustration and anger when things could not be managed.

Competitive and rivalrous feelings can, if they are too intense, become a serious impediment to the child's capacity

THINKING AND LEARNING

to learn. Being able to learn involves knowing that you need to learn and tolerating the discomfort of not knowing. The child who cannot tolerate this state of affairs, or who is made to feel stupid at not knowing, is already at a serious disadvantage.

William's parents were worried because although he was a bright little boy he could not concentrate in school and the teacher found him distracting and disruptive. He was not learning as well as might be expected. His parents decided to seek consultation at their local Child Guidance Clinic. In the course of the first meeting with the whole family one of the sisters showed her drawing to the psychotherapist who was talking to the parents. William, who was also drawing, immediately stopped what he was doing and came to take part in this exchange saying in a very grown up voice, "my sister can, sometimes, do very good drawings". William was showing how he could not bear to be left out or to allow his younger sister to have any attention or praise, as this made him fear he would lose what he believed was his superior status as the oldest boy. His intensely competitive feelings towards his sister, and his jealousy of the attention she was getting quickly distracted him from his own activity and prompted him to try in a rather false way to become grown-up like the therapist. One can see how difficult it would be for such a child to concentrate and to learn.

Difficulties in learning may arise for a multitude of reasons which have little to do with the child's innate capacity. Lack of concentration is a very common cause, although it must be remembered that the attention span of a child of six to seven is still quite limited. This is reflected in the daily timetables of most modern primary schools which give ample scope for different kinds of activities. Also children of different temperaments will at this stage show varying degrees of concentration and perseverance. An out-going, talkative child who is having to struggle with the urge to chat and socialise will find it much harder to sit down and work consistently at a task than a quieter, more introspective child.

If there is something upsetting going on at home, an illness in the family, or parents going through divorce, a child will be thrown off balance and the ability to take things in, to think or to concentrate will falter. Financial worries or fears of redundancy put parents under enormous stress, and this is bound to affect a six year old who is ordinarily alert and sensitive to his parents moods. For parents already under strain, to have a child showing problems at school can feel like the last straw, but it is too much to expect a child to carry on as though nothing is happening. Of course the problem may have arisen from a situation at school which the child is struggling to cope with by himself – for example a quarrel with a best friend or the sheer intensity of playground politics which may be getting the child down. More often than not these matters clear up – indeed it is sometimes better, though agonising, to allow time for your child to sort it out alone. At these times, perhaps all the parents can do is to be there to pick up the pieces, or bear the brunt of the child's temporary "bolshiness", clinginess, drop in work level or whatever. I think one of the most difficult things for parents at this stage when their child is becoming interested and involved in school life, is to bear the feelings of becoming less central and of being less in a position to do anything about some of the anxious moments the child has to negotiate. Mrs Lewis was recalling the period of enormous upheaval when the family moved to a new district and the two children, Ann aged six and Michael aged seven and a half had to go to a new school. Mrs Lewis was pleased in many ways with the school and had taken some trouble to prepare the children for the change. However she discovered on their first day that the girls and boys played separately during playtime which meant they could not meet and play together, at least for the time being, until they had settled and made some friends. The school remained firm that the children had to play separately, causing Mrs Lewis considerable anguish when she thought of them having to cope alone in the new environment. They did cope and after a period of uncertainty and a little unhappiness they both eventually came to be very happy in the school.

Sometimes difficulties in learning may affect one area of activity more than another and it is often unclear why this is happening. For example, William, the little boy mentioned above, was very good at reading; he was in fact way beyond the average for his age. However, he was very poor at arithmetic and at writing anything down on paper. In the meeting William spent a little time drawing and playing, though with frequent interruptions to check what his sisters were doing, but after a while he went and sat in a corner with his back to everyone, reading comics and chuckling loudly to himself from time to time. He seemed to withdraw his interest from everything going on in the room, and shut everyone out. His mother confirmed William's extraordinary ability to do this, to the point of aggravating her intensely when she wanted to draw his attention and he apparently did not hear. Of course to be able to be immersed in a story is a great asset and pleasure, but William seemed to be showing how he could use this capacity to control any feelings of uncertainty in an unfamiliar situation and appear to be very self confident and grown up.

The disadvantage for William in this way of coping with anxiety was demonstrated in the same meeting at the Clinic. He asked to go to the toilet and when one of the workers offered to show him the way he refused and said he knew the way. He went off with a great show of confidence but the worker who followed him found him wandering about looking very lost. For William admitting he didn't know was very difficult – perhaps it made him feel small and remind him too much of being a dependant child when he was trying so hard to be grown-up. It is possible to see how this pseudo-independent, "laid-back" picture of himself that William needed so desperately to present to the world would be put at risk if he engaged actively in the rigorous task of doing sums or committing himself to paper.

If your child's level of work or concentration deteriorates suddenly and dramatically it could be an indication that something is going on which needs to be investigated. For instance a child may be being bullied or may be frightened by a teacher's manner and be too scared to say anything. More seriously, it is not uncommon for a child who is being abused to display sudden learning difficulties as well as behavioural problems. It may be helpful to think of any such changes in the same way as a pain being an indication that all is not well physically. A continuous and mutually supportive relationship between school and parents will provide an invaluable forum where such matters can be discussed and the sort of intervention needed can be decided.

Learning to read

In the second year of school life, learning to read will continue to be the core of the curriculum. As has been stressed in the previous books in this series, there is a close connection between speech and reading. One of the very interesting facts that has come out of recent studies in learning processes is that children who by the age of three are familiar with the idea of rhyming words find learning to read easier at a later stage. This would reinforce the view that reading and singing nursery rhymes to your baby is not only fun but also a very important stage in the learning process. That the rhythms and cadences of mother's voice play a vital role in her baby's emotional state has been graphically shown on videos of recent experiments in psychology. If your child has been talked and listened to in very early infancy and read to later on he or she will be very "at home" with the notion of listening and making themselves understood which includes the wish to be heard and to understand. This will be the baseline from which your child will begin to learn to read. On coming into school at the age of five your child is faced with a new situation requiring more effort to be understood. Words and pronunciations which are idiosyncratic but perfectly well understood by the family may well leave teachers and classmates somewhat baffled. Stammering may also inhibit a child's capacity to make clear what he wants to say. Often by the age of six to seven such speech problems will have cleared up of their own accord but if they are persistent or acute it may be helpful to think what the difficulties are about.

Most children will be talking fluently by the time they are six though their vocabulary will be limited. Speaking now has the more purposeful aim of making a communication or expressing a thought, unlike the earlier stages when it was more about forming the words and identifying things, or giving a kind of commentary. The process of learning to read means going back into the slow lane, as it were, as children have to learn to recognise the printed symbols which represent the words they are using easily in speech. This is hard work and entails patience and perseverence on the child's part. By the time the seventh birthday comes around most children will be reading simple stories though not entirely fluently. In helping children to learn to read, teachers are careful to make sure they not only can read the letters but also have some understanding of what they are reading about. Some children show great facility in learning and memorising letters and words but this may mask an insecure understanding of the content. For this reason going slower sometimes makes more sense.

Books for children of this age tend to have a very clear construction – a beginning, a middle, and an end, which seems to reflect the need of children at this age to have a sense of continuity; of things "going on". Perhaps this is why many writers of fairy stories began their stories so precisely "Once upon a time ..." giving a feeling of pleasant anticipation, and ended with a satisfying "and they lived happily ever after". The simplicity of the construction makes the reading easier and also in itself accustoms the child to a sense of structure and completeness. Children at this age tend to have favourite books which they like to have read to them over and over again – often resisting a bored parent's attempts to get them interested in something new. One father recalled being asked to read the story of Peter Pan over and over again to his two young children. He also remembered with affection how quick they were to notice if he tried to skip a page or two!

Reading is an area of development which causes great anxiety for many parents – understandably as reading is so basic a necessity in life. Maria had just turned six when the school contacted her parents, Mr and Mrs Shaw, because they were worried that she seemed withdrawn and isolated at school. However in the course of a discussion about this with the teacher it became clear that Mrs Shaw was more concerned that Maria was not learning to read as well as she should. The teacher acknowledged that this was indeed the case but that they were not unduly worried about this at this stage. On further exploration with Mrs Shaw it came out that she herself had had considerable difficulty learning to read and she felt ashamed of this even though she had eventually managed to learn. She seemed almost convinced that Maria would have the same difficulties as she had had, and the way she said this conveyed deep anxiety and guilt that she had somehow transmitted the difficulties to her daughter, rather like a disease. When she was asked if she read stories to her daughter she eagerly said she did – Maria brought her reading book home every night from school and Mrs Shaw got her to read out of it! It was important for Mrs Shaw to recognise that her extreme anxiety about Maria's lack of progress was preventing her from being sensitive to Maria's unhappiness, and causing her to put extra pressure on her daughter. It was also painful for Mrs Shaw to consider that her anxiety and guilt may have been to do with the anger she felt about having a worrying child and which Maria undoubtedly sensed. A tense situation then built up around the whole issue of reading in which Maria's fears of being a source of disappointment to her parents escalated and contributed further to her difficulty in learning to read.

In these early stages when your child is concentrating on recognising the letters and words, following the story is more difficult. Having the opportunity to listen and take in the story as an adult reads is still a very important part of the learning process and will reinforce your child's wish to read for pleasure. Most primary schools have a period at the end of the day when the children sit in a group and are read to by the teacher. Such a provision comes from a recognition that being at school all day is very tiring for six year olds and like adults they need a chance to unwind and enjoy becoming absorbed in a good story. The most important way a parent can help their six year old's reading is to continue to read stories at home, especially as this experience has the added pleasure of a parent's lap to recall the comfort and security of not-so-distant babyhood.

Dyslexia

Dyslexia literally means "difficulty with words". It is commonly used to describe specific difficulties in learning to read. In origin it is a medical term, and reflects a view that problems with reading may have a physical cause. Hearing difficulties have been found in many cases of dyslexia. However there is considerable controversy among the medical profession, educationalists and psychologists about what dyslexia actually means and what the specific features of it are. For example the tendency to see letters back to front or to read words in the wrong order are thought to be symptoms of dyslexia. But some experts see those kind of features as part of the normal process of learning which seem to persist in some children. There are psychologists who see dyslexia primarily as a problem resulting from some emotional block. Many parents find it reassuring to have a name like "dyslexia" to put to their child's difficulty but this can then give rise to frustration and disappointment when the "experts" seem unable to cure it. It is perhaps important to know that educationalists and psychologists disagree about dyslexia and about how useful a term it is in their efforts to find ways of teaching which would help individual children. From the parents' point of view it is bewildering to be met with disparate views on something that causes them such great anxiety. Children with reading problems that seem acute or persistent may benefit from professional help and most schools have an Educational Psychologist who is there to explore such matters with worried parents.

Maths

Children vary in their ability to write and express themselves in stories. In the same way some children seem to find Maths a constant struggle while others move into this area easily and naturally. Why there should be these differences is puzzling and not very well understood.

It might be useful to think a little about the mental processes of doing arithmetic, and what those processes signify emotionally to a six year old who is now required to learn about numbers in a serious way. Mathematical ideas provoke a lot of anxiety – and why this should be so is also puzzling. One possibility is the way numbers represent relationships. The child has to learn to manipulate and change these when adding, subtracting, multiplying and dividing and this new power may have anxieties connected with it. Some children seem to tackle such a task with a will while others appear to be rather fearful of doing this. These children may show considerable reluctance or lack of interest in maths. Many adults feel the same kind of wariness towards maths and occasionally this is conveyed to the child.

The influence of the parents is illustrated by a teacher who recalled a little boy in one of her classes who was a slow learner, though not unintelligent. To the teacher's surprise this child showed an unexpected facility with numbers – adding up, substracting etc. When she quizzed him about this she discovered that the boy's father gambled on horses and the boy would watch and listen to his father calculating odds, winnings and losings, divisions between members of a syndicate etc etc. Thus, by the time he was six the child was already familiar with numbers and unafraid of manipulating them.

By the time they are six most children can keep in their minds the idea of a number as a group of objects. A group of 5 and 10 may be easier to grasp because they know about having 5 and 10 fingers. They have played some nursery games on their fingers such as "One, two, three four five, once I caught a fish alive", or "This little piggy went to market". The number two may be especially significant because there are two parents, and three may remind a child of 2 parents and 1 child.

Children at this stage of development still tend to think in concrete images that refer to their immediate world and to themselves. A mother recalled with amusement how her daughter aged nearly six, upon being told they were moving house and they would need her help, very quickly assured her mother that she could probably manage to carry the door-knobs but "could Daddy carry the doors?" Adults are so accustomed to thinking in the metaphorical sense of moving house that it is startling to realise that a child may be thinking very literally about "moving house".

At this age large numbers are often equated with power and strength, and children can sometimes be heard talking of hundreds or thousands, not because they have a concept of a hundred or a thousand but because in so doing they can feel the "bigness" of the number themselves.

A little boy, Martin, was trying to describe to his teacher how big a dinosaur was, and he was also trying very hard to impress her with its size. He stumbled a bit over the length – he reckoned about 3, 4, 5 metres maybe and he managed to get to a reasonable approximation. However the height of the dinosaur was much more of a problem for him – he looked at the ceiling, pursed his lips as he struggled to imagine what it might be. He finally came up with "about 4 or 5 feet", and this was clearly meant to bowl his teacher over. What was significant about Martin's hesitation was not only getting the proportions wrong, but the fact that he himself was a small child for his age, the smallest in the class, and this was a considerable source of discomfort to him. It was as though his conflicts about his own height together with his longing to be important to his teacher interfered with his capacity to imagine freely the height of the dinosaur.

How can parents help?

We have seen throughout this series how your child's learning experience begins from birth and how continuing development is closely related to feelings, conflicts, relationships with the parents and within the family. Now that the more formal education is in the hands of the teachers, parents often feel at a loss to know how they can best go on helping their child. Teaching methods have changed a great deal and as we have seen the children at this stage learn much by doing things – like painting pictures, making models, doing number work with shapes, rods and containers – and this can make it more difficult for parents to help directly. Also teachers sometimes feel concerned that if the parents do too much work at home with the child, they will force the pace and thus cause anxiety or resentment in the child. So what can parents do? It is of course important for children to know that parents are interested in what they are doing at school and that they will be pleased with pictures brought home for example, or a carefully constructed, if rather gluey model, or the latest reading book. If they want to show how well they can read then it is important to find some time for this. Continuing to

THINKING AND LEARNING

read stories to your child will foster an easy familiarity with words and books, while the sharing of everyday activities like shopping, cooking, woodwork will give him or her the pleasure of showing off a new-found skill in counting, weighing or measuring.

Many schools take classes on outings to a local museum or art gallery, or to the park for nature studies but in these days of tight budgets and staff shortages such "extras" become harder for schools to provide. Parents can help a great deal by taking their child on such outings. Not only does the child have the fun of a family trip, but also has an added experience which will enrich work in school and which can be drawn on to contribute to class discussions.

Open evenings at school, when the childrens' work is on show, or school plays, which all the children will have had a hand in somewhere, are important events to a six year old; making the effort to go to these (and sometimes it is an effort, especially on a cold night after a day's work or if you have to make special arrangements) will pay dividends because in letting your child know that their efforts are noticed and valued you will reinforce their confidence and their motivation to go on. Children who know that the work they do at school is valued by parents, even if mother and father do not know exactly what goes on, are more likely to feel happy and eager to do well there than children whose parents are dismissive or too busy.

CHAPTER TWO

NEW RELATIONSHIPS

Adjustments

If all has gone well your six year old will now be happily settled at school, no longer the youngest there, and forging ahead with all the new experiences that school has to offer.

While the child's emotional base remains firmly in the family, the centre of interest is starting to shift to the exciting world of the classroom and playground. The separation from mother which began already in the first year of life continues as our six year old becomes involved in new relationships with teachers and classmates. From now on there will be increasingly large areas of your child's life that can only be glimpsed at by the parents and from which they are excluded.

This shift will make emotional demands on your child and also on you as parents. At this stage the intensity of the small child's relationships with mother and father changes in quality as some of the rawness of his feelings towards them lessens. The wishes and longings of babyhood, sometimes expressed for example, in the toddler's fierce determination that he or she will one day marry mummy or daddy, are gradually recognised as unattainable, disappointment is overcome, and the child is spurred on to make his or her own relationships.

There may be even more of a sense for parents of losing "their baby", and this can be disconcerting and painful. All steps forward involve change and a sense of loss – loss of a status quo, a kind of relationship, a way of being which was there before and was familiar but now has to be given up. One of the adjustments a parent has to make in these early years at school is being no longer the sole authority and provider in the child's life. Much of the mother's identity especially has been necessarily invested in her role as the central figure in her child's life. For a single or separated parent, the adjustment may be particularly difficult.

One mother recalled how she had enjoyed sharing her interest in birds with her small son David, showing him pictures and naming them with him. One day when he was nearly seven he came home and announced he wasn't interested in birds any more. Understandably disappointed and hurt, she asked him why. "It's not cool," he said. Clearly in playground talk certain things were "cool" and therefore "O.K." and others definitely weren't, like birdwatching with your Mum!

There are bonuses too, of course. For both child and parents, the seventh year of life, with its greater separation from family, and the increasing diversity of the child's interests bring with it a sense of liberation from the turmoil of the toddler stage.

As part of this process children may want to keep home and school separate and maintain a kind of privacy about an outside life which they are struggling to get to grips with. Parents sometimes express hurt and exasperation when their six year old shows a marked reluctance to talk about the day at school. "He never tells me anything" is a frequent complaint and it is indeed frustrating when the information gleaned is absolutely nil. "How was school today?" . . . "All right." "What did you do today?" . . . "Nothing much." Of course there may be other reasons for this; your child may simply be dead tired and just not in the humour to expound – a school day can be exhausting for a six-year old. It may spring from a recognition that you as the parents have your private life from which he or she is excluded and it's an assertion of the right to have the same. If there is a younger brother or sister at home with mother it may be an expression of feelings of jealousy about that relationship going on at home. If there is something troubling your child at school which he or she cannot or will not talk about, it may come to the parents' notice as an eating problem or a sleep problem, or as a bout of clinginess; often there is nothing particularly wrong – just a growing awareness on the part of your child that problems have to be confronted on his or her own.

For the majority of children these changes in their internal life tend to come in fits and starts, as they did in the toddler stages, veering between self-sufficiency to clinging babyishness. It is important to remember that a six year old's confidence is not very securely established and can be easily shaken. Now, as much of the tempestuousness and turbulence of feelings hitherto directed towards the parents is suppressed, the relationships with schoolmates and teachers become more central to the child's life.

The teacher

For a child whose parents can tolerate the feelings of sadness at the loss of their "at home" child and take pleasure in the eagerness to get to grips with the outside world, being six and happily established in the school environment can bring with it a sense of exhilarating liberation. In the relationship to the teacher, your child will bring to bear many of the facets of the relationships and experiences at home with parents and brothers and sisters. It is not uncommon to hear a six year old in a forgetful moment, addressing the teacher as "Mummy". This may evoke pangs of jealousy for many mothers but it is also an indication that the child does feel settled and "at home" in the classroom.

However, your six year old will also experience a greater underlying sense that different demands are being made. Teachers and parents all expect the first few days or weeks at school to be a stressful time, but by the time a child goes into the second year class, the adult's attitudes have subtly changed. Going to school is no longer seen as an achievement in itself; now results are expected; there is a more purposeful approach to learning and more pressure is put on the child.

This shift may bring with it some anxiety, but if it is done with tact and care it will also encourage children to take themselves and the work seriously.

It is during this time at school that children begin to come up against the possibility of failure as well as success. They have to come to terms with the idea that improvement and achievements do not come from indulgent adults but from their own efforts. More demands are made on six year olds by the teacher to fit in with classroom rules, and as each teacher brings a different atmosphere to her or his class, the six year old has to adapt. For these kinds of reasons, the teacher, however kindly, may seem at times even to an eager six year old, severe or unpredictable.

Perhaps this first real encounter with the unpredictability of the outside world in relation to the teacher contributes to the tendency at this age for children to maintain a belief in their minds that their teacher is a kind of fixture in the classroom; even that she actually lives there. In this way they can imagine that she "belongs" to them. It is very common for six year olds to be amazed and excited to see "teacher" in the street, or in the supermarket, perhaps with spouse or children. This may be one reason why children round about this age can become very unsettled if their teacher is absent through illness, or leaves to have a baby. The extent to which this can happen was evident on one occasion when a teacher was taken seriously ill quite suddenly. In the urgency to provide another teacher at short notice for the class, the children were not told what had happened. Over the next week, several children were absent with unexplained stomach pains, and one mother was called in to take her child home as she was complaining of headaches and nausea. It was very striking indeed how the childrens' anxiety and sudden feelings of insecurity seemed to be manifested in physical ailments.

Most parents are well aware of how disrupting it can be for a child to have a change of teacher – just as it is for adults to have a change of manager or colleague. Sean was a child who found starting school very difficult. He would cling to his mother and cry desperately as though he would fall apart if separated from her. This indeed made it hard for her to leave him in the mornings. Sean's first teacher, who happened to be a man, proved to be patient and understanding but also quite firm in enabling mother and child to separate, although this took quite a time. Perhaps the fact that his first teacher in school was a man made it especially difficult for Sean. Over the course of the year Sean made a very good relationship to his teacher and, although his difficulties in school were by no means over, the immediate problem of his reluctance to be parted from his mother eased. However there then came the time when Sean had to leave this teacher and move on to the six year old class and make a new relationship. Fortunately both the school and Sean's mother remained fully aware of his difficulties and could therefore prepare themselves for the possibility of a setback. They could also take steps to prepare Sean for the change – for example letting him know who his new teacher would be and arranging for him to meet her and visit her classroom. The causes of Sean's extreme anxiety about separating from his mother were complex and probably not fully understood. What seemed important was that his anxiety was taken seriously and thought was given both by the school and Sean's mother to making it more manageable.

Jane has already been mentioned in a previous book in this series as a child who always found changes and separation a problem. True to form, at the age of six she still could not leave her mother in the mornings to go to school without a scene, although her mother had assured herself, by talking to the teacher, that Jane was all right once she was in school. Jane seemed to be making her mother feel guilty for being so hard-hearted as to send her away, as though she was sending her to a terrible place and making Jane unhappy. Although Jane's mother understood this to some extent, she could not help at times being exasperated with her daughter and at such times did indeed send Jane to school amid scenes of angry confrontation. Jane's mother had the good fortune to have a friendly neighbour whose child went to the same school and who was in fact a close friend of Jane's, and she was able to come to an arrangement to share the burden of taking the two girls to school.

The kind of state Jane got into about going to school is not uncommon and is distressing for any parent. It is also hard for the parent to go on being firm in such circumstances. If Jane's mother had given in too easily to her daughter's distress she would not have been helping her child in the long run to overcome her difficulties in leaving mother and the comfortable familiarity of home. Sometimes it really does feel like pushing the fledgling out of the nest – part of the hard work of being a parent at such times is having to judge when it is better to push the child a little, and when to make room for the clingy feelings the child might have.

If the child has particular difficulties with parents at home before going to school, the likelihood is that adjustment to school and teachers will be more problematic. Ali, aged nearly seven, was finding it impossible to settle at school, and his teacher was finding him very hard to manage. He was aggressive to teachers and children alike, he had no friends, and he could not concentrate, so his performance was poor. His parents tended to be inconsistent in their handling of him. Mrs Matheou was a quiet woman who did not seem to be able to say no to her son, or thwart him in any way. She seemed very worried about arousing his anger and would get him to do things by wheedling, cajoling or bribing him. His older sister was often required to assist her mother in this and mostly took a back seat uncomplainingly. Mrs Matheou often complained in a resigned but ineffectual way that Ali never listened to her. Mr Matheou was impatient with his wife, and pointed out that he never had any trouble with Ali, and in a way this was true. In fact Ali seemed rather frightened of his father who, although he never raised his voice, could almost control Ali with a look. Mrs Matheou therefore frequently resorted to threatening Ali with his father's discipline when he was being disobedient. It is not difficult to imagine how hard it would be for Ali to make any adjustments to the ordinary demands made on him at school by his usually female teachers. He did not know how to relate to one person, his teacher, who was both helpful and kindly towards him, but who also insisted on work being done and rules being observed. He could not tolerate the rivalry with the other children in the class, so accustomed was he to taking precedence over his sister.

In this transitional phase between home and outside world, therefore, the teacher is a rather awesome figure who nevertheless represents a source of security and stability. Perhaps this is one of the reasons why most children want to be special and noticed by her or him. This is a carry-over from home where siblings vied for mother or father's attention and secretly wanted to be the favourite. But now the wish to be 'teacher's pet' has to be managed in a different way, and to some extent suppressed as the child has to make room for many classmates. An only child may find this more difficult than a child who has had the experience of having to share with siblings at home. If there is a good relationship between child and teacher, and between his parents and the school the child's feelings of jealousy and rivalry will be mitigated by feelings of admiration for his teacher as a recognised source of knowledge and helpfulness.

However, children and teachers being human, their relationships may not be all plain sailing! Teachers as well as children have their "off" days, and part of the process of learning about the outside world is coming up against other people's unfamiliar quirks and personalities. If the child's basic relationship with the teacher is good, he can probably weather moments of feeling slighted or overlooked by a busy teacher and even days when his teacher seems irritable or less patient than usual. More serious is when a child and a teacher just don't seem to hit it off. If this happens – and it does from time to time – it is very important to talk to the child and try to find out what is going wrong and whether anything can be done. It may be important also to talk to the teacher but if this feels too difficult then it may be useful to have a word with the head teacher.

Many classrooms contain children from different ethnic and cultural groups and a good teacher will use this situation to enrich and broaden the children's knowledge of the world. But it can also bring problems. This is particularly so where the parents do not speak English or where family values seem very different. Most Education Departments make provision for interpreters to be available, and special English classes are usually held for children from families where English is not the spoken tongue at home. A six year old is now made very aware of differences which exist between families, and groups; differences in language, interests, religion – often just differences in the way things are done. Most teachers try very hard not to be partisan in political, racial or religious attitudes. However it is quite impossible for a teacher not to express a great deal about him or herself by dress, manner of speech or chance remarks, and children of this age are quick to register these things in an adult who is very important to them.

In dealing with all these issues it is evident that mutually helpful and supportive communication between school and home will greatly enhance your child's ability to settle down and get the most out of school life. Just as you as the parent need to be kept informed of what is going on in school and how your six year old is doing, so the teacher also needs to know about events at home which might affect your child's behaviour and capacity to learn.

School friends

Standing in the playground of an infants' school, one is

immediately struck by how the children at this age seem naturally to separate off into single-sex groups to play. A group of boys is noisily playing "cops and robbers" which involves a lot of running and chasing with raucous siren and gunshot noises. A group of girls play at mothers and fathers, equally noisily and with much intense jostling for position and roles. There seem to be some neutral games like "stick in the mud" or "hide and seek" in which girls and boys might join in together but on the whole there does seem to be a natural inclination for children around about this age, when left to themselves, to play in groups of their own sex. This often continues throughout the so-called "latency" period until sexual feelings and interest in the opposite sex emerge again at puberty.

Another striking feature of the games of six to seven year olds is how much time is spent working out rules and hierarchies. Often this process seems to be the main point of the game. One mother reported with amusement watching her six year old daughter playing with a friend, setting up a house. A great deal of time was spent trying to decide where the television aerial should go and which way it should point. Why this particular feature should be so important is not clear, but it did seem to indicate that what the two girls were doing was working out how to negotiate, compromise, deal with rivalry and their wishes to have their own way etc.

In the game of mothers and fathers in the Wendy House, there was a bossy little girl, swinging from the rafters, and insisting she was mother, or possibly big sister. The others were required to sit behind upturned tables being children, one of whom was "the baby". Nothing much actually happened in the game except that "mother" or "big sister" was an autocratic, overbearing figure giving orders in a loud voice. It was not long before there was rebellion; the "baby" had clearly had enough and was making a bid to be "mother", and for a while pandemonium broke loose, before a precarious agreement was reached and a new "mother" restored order.

What are we to make of these games? Clearly many intense feelings are around and by no means "latent"! There seemed to be a need for all the participants to have a chance to identify with a powerful figure "mother" or "police chief", in which role the child could play out wishes to boss and control friends. In the girls' game, being willing to be the "baby" sucking a thumb, seemed to be a way of recalling babyhood, which was quite quickly repudiated as being too limited a role – babies can't do much! The game may also have provided a forum where the girls could express safely their anger and jealousy towards real babies who receive the special care from mother which they had had to give up not so long ago. It is striking too how often the "mother" or "police chief" figure is portrayed as very authoritarian, almost cruel. In such games the children seem to need to express anxieties about being at the mercy of such figures, but also in playing at being these figures they are learning about their own bossy, controlling feelings and how to manage them in a group.

Not only do children at this age begin to separate into groups of their own sex, but what also seems to happen is a quite active and often vociferous rejection of the opposite sex.

> "What are little boys made of?
> Slugs and snails and puppy-dogs tails;
> Thats what little boys are made of.
> What are little girls made of?
> Sugar and spice and all things nice;
> That's what little girls are made of."

"Boys are rude, noisy, dirty," say the girls. "Girls are sissy, stupid, cry-babies," say the boys. The urge to retreat into his or her own sexual group may have the function of allowing the child to consolidate and "practise" their identity as a member of that group. There may also be a way whereby all the character traits which the group feels uncomfortable about or a bit ashamed of, are attributed, with much scorn, to the opposite sex. The well-known rhyme quoted above is loaded with female "chauvinism" where all the "yukky" feelings are lodged in the boys, but the slugs, snails and puppy dogs tails may contain an allusion to the girls' awareness and wariness of the boys' more obvious genitals.

There is another difference between boys and girls which begins to manifest itself around this age, and that is the tendency among girls to have "a best friend" to the exclusion of others, while boys seem to have a "best friend" but more often in the context of a group. These friendships sometimes last for a long time and become very intense – the two children become inseparable. For some children friendships seem to come and go but may nevertheless be very intense and such children appear to be in a constant turmoil of on/off relationships often to the bewilderment and exasperation of the parents.

To some extent these differences between boys and girls and between individual children are perfectly normal, and often due to the temperament of the child. The children who seem not to have or be able to make friends with whom they can go through the vicissitudes of a relationship in an ordinary way are more worrying. These children usually come to the notice of the teachers in the playground. He or she might be a "loner" who is isolated from the groups, or a child who is teased by the other children. It is sometimes the child who tries to become a member of a group but seems only to succeed in aggravating the others or else becomes physically aggressive. There can be any number of reasons why these difficulties arise for a particular child – sometimes quite simple ones like a cultural or social problem which is readily identifiable. Or there may be some more deep-seated cause in the child or the family which may need professional help. A good school with sensitive staff will be on the alert to identify a child who is having problems making friends and will want to co-operate with the parents in trying to alleviate the problem. But it is as well to be aware that children normally are sociable – thought and attention need to be given to a child who is particularly isolated and lonely.

CHAPTER THREE

THE SIX YEAR OLD AND THE FACTS OF LIFE

One of the ways in which your six year old is changing is the way of expressing involvement in the life around – less by bodily language, gestures or enactment and more by observation, questions and thought. Around this age your child wants to know, find out, explore and be given explanations for how and why things are as they are.

Maxim Gorky, writing at the turn of the century in Russia, recalls, in the opening chapter of his book, 'My Childhood', the traumatic experience of witnessing within the same hour the death of his father and the birth of his brother. Later, he was present at the funeral of his father, and gives a vivid picture of the scene through the eyes of a child of five.

"I stood on the a slippery heap of sticky mud and

THE SIX YEAR OLD AND THE FACTS OF LIFE

looked down into the pit where my father's coffin had been lowered. At the bottom was a lot of water, and a few frogs. Two of them had succeeded in climbing on to the yellow coffin lid. My grandmother, myself, a policeman who looked soaked to the skin, and two men with spades who were evidently in a very bad mood, had gathered round the grave. A warm rain, as fine as delicate beads, began to fall gently on us.

"'Fill it in,' said the policeman as he walked away.

"Grandmother burst into tears and hid her face in her shawl. The gravediggers, bent double, began piling the earth into the grave at great speed. Water squelched. The frogs jumped off the coffin and tried to escape up the sides, but were thrown back by clods of earth. . . . Grandmother took me by the hand and led me to a distant church surrounded by a great number of dark crosses.

"'Why don't you cry?' she asked when we left the cemetery, 'you ought to cry.'

"'I don't want to.' I replied.

"'Well, you'd better not if you don't want to,' she said softly. . . .

"Afterwards we rode in a droshky along a broad and very muddy street lined with houses painted deep red. I asked Grandmother;

"'Will the frogs get out?'

"'No, they don't stand a chance, God help them!'

"Neither my mother nor my father ever mentioned the name of God so often and with such familiarity."

Gorky was taken by his mother and Grandmother to live in the house of his maternal grandfather which he describes as "choked by a fog of mutual hostility". His appalling experiences there were made just bearable by the large, comforting presence of his Grandmother with whom he shared a bed and who answered his questions and explained the unexplainable to him.

Mercifully, most of our six year olds do not come against such facts of life, so brutally, but the description above demonstrates a child's capacity for acute observation of what is going on around him, and to his vulnerability and fear of being overwhelmed by events, as the frogs were by the clods of earth. The child Gorky, in asking his question about the frogs, may have been was also wanting to know what was happening to his father underneath the clods and expressing some of his despair about him not being able to get out.

Old age

It is not unusual for children at this age to become preoccupied with some particular aspect of life, like age, death, illness. The question of where babies come from will usually have come up long before the age of six – the enquiries now will be more searching – "how did the baby get into Mummy?" for example – and this will be discussed later on in this chapter.

Six is an age of endless questions, some easy to answer, some impossible, some tricky, some just embarrassing. "Why is Auntie Muriel so fat?" one mother recalled her son asking when barely out of earshot of Auntie Muriel. "Why has Gran got such a big nose?" Jane was heard to ask her mother. The explanation that Gran had fallen on her nose when playing tennis in her youth prompted thoughtful remarks from Jane about the idea of Gran being at one time young enough to play tennis. Children at this age are fascinated by the realisation that their parents were once actually children too and can begin to apprehend the reality of the relationships to Grandparents. Photographs of their parents as children are of great interest, and can help children to understand a little more about growing old, the passage of time, and, what is of even more interest to them, the realisation of there being a time when they did not exist. When Sarah was just six she asked her mother where she was before she was born. Her mother replied that she was just a little egg. Sarah persisted – "no, I mean where was I before that?" "Well, you were . . . well, nothing!" Sarah was horrified – it was very hard for her to really take this in.

Louise at six and a half, was taken to visit some elderly friends of her grandparents – they were in their early eighties. Louise was rather quiet and shy to begin with but eventually whispered to her father "would she be allowed to see round the house?" The couple kindly agreed and when they went into the bedroom, Louise, now a little bolder, asked them if they still slept in the same bed, much to the consternation of her parents. Fortunately, the couple were aware that Louise was not being rude, but was genuinely intrigued and curious about their life together.

Old people seem awe-inspiring to small children and the physical aspects of old age will be immediately noticeable because they are so different from their own bodies, so much so that they may show reluctance to go near to a very old person.

David had been referred to the Child Guidance Clinic because he seemed unable to make relationships with either his teachers or with classmates. He was a bright boy but was cut off from the world around him and seemed to live in a world of his own. In one of his therapy sessions he came and stood very close to the therapist, staring at her hair. When she asked what he was seeing he replied that he was thinking that she was old because she had grey hairs. In the next session the therapist, following something David had been doing with string, tying things together, was talking to him about how things, but also people, became attached to one another. David came again and stood very close to the therapist, this time staring at her face very intently. He said to her that he was thinking that she was old but in a different way. When she asked him what he meant, he said that she had wrinkles and that people got wrinkles when they were old but young people didn't have wrinkles. What was actually very touching about this interchange was that in the moment of noticing a real difference between himself and the therapist, and talking about it with her, David was also making a connection with her, as he had been making connections in his play with the string.

Talking about death

The illness or death of a grandparent may stimulate a great deal of curiosity as well as anxiety about their parents' possible deaths. Usually at this age children are unable to imagine their own deaths. At a difficult emotional time like the death of a close relative, it may be hard to face questions about it which may seem rather stark. Many six year olds will be able to sense quickly when and when not to ask questions, but refusing to answer such questions, or to talk about the dead person may give the child the feeling of not being supposed to know, or to share in the sadness. Parents are often unsure whether for example, a child of this age should be allowed to go to a funeral – perhaps because they believe it would not be good to witness parents and other adults crying or in a sad state. If the person who has died was a close and loved relative, like a grandparent, the child would undoubtedly feel it as a cruel exclusion to be denied the opportunity to take part in the mourning.

It is a great mistake to think that children at this age "don't notice" when an event like this happens. Most parents would want to see their children grow up to be sensitive to other people's feelings – allowing them to have some share in upsetting family events like a death or a serious illness, and even to be of some comfort to a grieving parent, will help them to feel not only that their contribution and participation is important and valued but also that their own relationship to the dead or ill person is recognised and taken seriously.

Sometimes the child's curiosity about particular issues like death seem to come out of the blue, as it were. It may have been stimulated by seeing something on the television or hearing of a death in someone else's family. The classroom pet, usually a hampster or guinea pig, is a great source of information and discovery about "births, marriages and deaths". When the death is not so immediate, the child will perhaps feel freer to ask questions like "what does a dead person look like?" or "what happens to them when they're in the ground?"

etc. On the whole it is wise to answer such questions as straightforwardly and honestly as possible.

One mother was more than a little bemused about the questions her daughter Jenny, who was just six, kept asking; along the lines of, "when you die, who will have our house?" or "when you die, can I have that big yellow brooch in your jewel box?" Fortunately this mother had a sense of humour, although she did confess to being a little hurt by her daughters persistent thoughts of her death, not to say alarmed by Jenny's apparently mercenary attitude. It seems likely that Jenny was in her own way trying to master her underlying anxiety about the idea of her loved mother dying, but perhaps also testing out to some extent how her mother would react to such questions. Of course, like all little girls Jenny may also have been feeling rivalrous with her mother and could well have had wishful thoughts of having father all to herself.

Illness

If there is a serious illness in the family, like cancer for example, whether of a parent or a brother or sister or cousin, the question of how much, and when, to talk to a child of this age about it vexes many parents. One thing that can be said with certainty is that it does no good to maintain a pretence that everything is absolutely fine, in the face of clear evidence to the contrary. Children become disturbed if their accurate perceptions that "something is going on" are persistently denied – they may become distrustful of adults generally, but even more seriously, distrustful of their own ability to see and to know. The child may feel compelled to go along with the pretence and secrecy in order to be approved of, and sometimes this may lead to an inhibition of intellectual curiosity in other areas. Also in such an atmosphere the child will come to believe there is no friendly ear to hear the distress and upset about the illness.

Parents may behave in a secretive way about such issues for several reasons; it may be a mistaken belief that they are thus sparing the child unnecessary upset – they may then need to ask themselves the question whether they are in reality avoiding having to face the child's distress as well as their own. In the long run it is more beneficial to the child to acknowledge the reality of the situation, as far as possible, and to establish an atmosphere in which the child feels free to ask the questions when ready. If, as is often the case with an illness like cancer, the prognosis is uncertain it is really difficult to know what to say when the question in everyone's mind, not least the child's, is "will Mummy, or Daddy, die?" To say merely "yes" would seem too brutal and stark, even if it is actually true; to say "no, of course not" if you actually don't know, would be untruthful and seem to promise something you can't deliver. Perhaps the best that parents can do in such a distressing situation, is to acknowledge their own uncertainty, as well as their hopes and thus be available when their children need to express theirs.

Sexuality and birth

Curiosity about anatomical differences is evident even in young toddlers, say at bathtime or watching each other pee. At the age of six, though sometimes earlier, children will sometimes make more serious explorations of each others bodies. A game of "doctors and nurses" is always a useful way of satisfying such curiosity, or a game of "rudies" or "touching wees". A certain amount of such activity is normal and it is probably not worth making a fuss about it. If a child seems constantly or obsessively to be demonstrating such behaviour, and alarming other children with it, that would be cause for serious concern.

It is a perennial problem for parents to know how to respond to their child's searching questions about sexual matters. The "where do babies come from?" question has probably come up before. Up till now answers like – it grows in Mummy's tummy . . . etc. etc. will have been enough, but by now the child will not be completely satisfied with that! Children invariably have their own theories about what sexual intercourse is all about – indeed they may know at an unconscious level and, by asking questions, are beginning to seek confirmation as well as information. But their ideas may be distorted, sometimes amusingly so, perhaps by wishful thinking, about how it should be. One father recalled putting his two children to bed, aged four and six, and being asked by the four year old how the baby got into mummy's tummy. Father stalled, saying he would tell him about it another day. The little boy persisted and his six year old sister in a wearied voice said "we might as well tell him now daddy, or he'll just go on and on about it". She then provided her own explanation – "daddy feeds mummy something – I don't know what it is but it has a lot of fibre in it!"

It was probably not a coincidence that the little four

THE SIX YEAR OLD AND THE FACTS OF LIFE

year old had chosen bedtime as a moment to ask his father the question. Jenny, the little girl mentioned earlier, had been ill in bed with high temperatures and feverishness during which time she had been allowed into the parents' bed. On one of these occasions she had been so restless that her father had decamped into Jenny's empty bed to get some sleep. During one of these moments of affectionate intimacy, and perhaps with the thought of being in father's place, Jenny was able to ask her mother about what she and daddy did together to make babies. Her mother answered with as much information as she thought Jenny was seeking and no more, leaving it to Jenny to ask more if she wanted to. After some thought Jenny said "but you don't do that at your wedding, do you, because that would be rude?"

The embarrassment and hesitation that many parents feel when faced with questions about sexuality probably springs from the fact that it comes so near to their own sexual life which they suspect, rightly, the child is intensely curious about. Undoubtedly your child, in asking these questions, is not only seeking information he or she is also seeking to get to grips with the unpalatable idea that mummy and daddy might be getting up to such things in bed. A good rule of thumb is perhaps to grasp the nettle as Jenny's mother did and explain simply what occurs during sexual intercourse, if that is what the child is asking, and leave it at that. If and when a child wants to know more, he or she will ask. It is important to be straight and honest with children – an ordinarily observant six year old will quickly twig if you are spinning a story – but it is also important to respect the child's privacy and to guard against over-exposure. Flooding the child with too much information may cause anxious embarrassment and lead to a reluctance to ask more questions later on. Some things are just too strong and disturbing for the mind of a young child of this age to cope with – for example witnessing parental intercourse or the birth of a baby – and they need to be shielded from such events.

Mrs Robinson was a mother bringing up two children on her own, having separated from her husband when the children were quite small. Life was a struggle and she relied quite heavily on the older child, Simon, to talk to and confide in, on day to day matters. Simon seemed to respond to this by becoming a rather grown up little boy but he also had worrying symptoms like wetting the bed and finding it difficult to get on well with other children of his age. When he was round about seven Simon began to bombard his mother with questions, mostly about sex, babies and menstruation. Mrs Robinson was particularly disconcerted that he would ask these questions at inappropriate times, like when in the check-out queue at the supermarket, or on the bus. His manner when asking was overbearing and demanding and Mrs Robinson felt very confused about how to deal with this. If she answered him he would ask more, and she was aware of feeling extremely angry with him for putting her in such an awkward position. It seemed likely that Simon was not, on these occasions, primarily concerned with obtaining information, but rather engaged in doing something to his mother – making her feel uncomfortable and angry. When Mrs Robinson tried to answer Simon's questions – against her better judgement – it made matters worse. Perhaps what Simon was really seeking was a firm response from his mother

THE SIX YEAR OLD AND THE FACTS OF LIFE

that he could wait till a more suitable moment – which would be a reassuring demonstration that she could and would protect herself from Simon's intrusiveness. His mother's tendency to treat Simon as though he was her companion or partner may have stimulated exciting thoughts that his earlier toddler wishes to get rid of father and have mother to himself may actually be coming true. But his worrying symptoms also suggested that Simon felt uncomfortable and frightened about this kind of relationship with her, in that he was not being given enough space to be a child and, as such, protected from his mother's adult needs.

The birth of another baby into the family will undoubtedly stimulate curiosity and questions, not only about where the baby came from but how it develops in the womb, how it eats (food and feeding is never far from a young child's thoughts) what it does in there and so on. They will be fascinated to feel the baby moving and kicking. Their worries and anxieties about the well-being of the baby and their mother may increase as the birth becomes imminent, though the form these anxieties take may be startling to an adult. One father recalled talking to his two children, then four and a half and six about the coming baby and how, to begin with, it would just sleep and feed most of the time and wouldn't bother them hardly at all. He went on to prepare them for the difficult days when the baby would be crawling around interfering with their toys and being more of a nuisance to them. In a pause in the conversation the six year old asked "will the baby have a head?" The child was clearly more worried at this point that the baby would arrive all in one piece.

Dangers

How to protect a child from danger is always a worry for parents, particularly now that the child is making a bid for more independence in a world that seems to become more and more hazardous. They do have to learn to cope with busy streets and a six year old will be learning from the parents' example. At this age children are not capable of judging the distance and speed of oncoming cars very accurately. Nor can they be relied on to exercise the necessary care if a best friend is spotted across the road – any sense of reality and danger is likely to desert them in their eagerness to get to the friend.

It almost goes without saying that children at this age should be warned against getting into strange cars, or going with people they don't know – how to do it without being too alarmist is a question many parents ask themselves. It may be better to err on the side of being alarmist if it will impress on the child the need for caution and thus prevent him getting into dangerous situations. It is vital that a child feels able to say no to what may seem like kindly offers of a lift or sweets – this means not worrying too much about being rude to an adult. A child who has had the experience within the family of "nos" and refusals being taken seriously will, by the age of six or seven, feel confident and comfortable about expressing likes and dislikes. Similarly, the child will be able to understand now that what is appropriate physical contact within the family may not be appropriate from a comparative stranger and again he should feel able to say "no".

THE SIX YEAR OLD AND THE FACTS OF LIFE

Child abuse

Child abuse is very much in the news these days and it is disquieting that it is probably more common than we would like to think. Small childrens' bodies are attractive and cuddly and it is right and natural that parents should express love for their child with hugs and caresses. It would be sad if a parent felt inhibited from such demonstrations of affection for fear of going too far or being called abusive. But it does happen in families, and a child who is grossly interfered with by a relative is put in an impossible position. He or she may feel unable to speak about it through fear, guilt, or a sense of loyalty. It more often happens that the child communicates distress and confusion by mood and behaviour changes, often quite startling, say from being content and relaxed to tearful, irritable, or withdrawn. Teachers at school may notice that the child's work deteriorates significantly, or the child shows sexualised behaviour towards other children. It is important to take such symptoms seriously and to try and find out the cause. A confidential talk with the child's teacher or school head may help and most Local Authorities have Child Protection Teams and Child Guidance Services where professional help is available.

Where does God live?

The six year old, now established at school, will begin to realise that religious faith takes many forms and that other childrens' experience may be vastly different from their own. In most schools in England some form of religious instruction is obligatory, though wide scope is given to the form that instruction might take as the school may include children from various ethnic backgrounds.

Children now have to learn to encompass the reality that people believe very different things, and at this stage will grapple with this problem in relation to the adults who are most significant to them, their parents and teachers, who may now be perceived to hold different views on religious matters. Most parents of children of this age will have had the experience of finding it difficult to answer questions like "do you believe in God?" or "what does God look like?" Part of the problem for parents stems both from the child's lingering expectation that parents should know everything and from the parents hovering wish to be that omniscient God-like person.

Religious questions highlight emotional realities which are a source of great anxiety – the possibility that adults disagree (often globally and very violently) and for reasons which may seem incomprehensible to a six year old. The question for him might come down to "whose side am I on?" (a feature which is also much in evidence in games at this age), in which the immediate conflict is the need to be approved of and accepted by parents and teacher, who may hold different religious views. Underneath this, deeper conflicts are touched on; for example the real need that children of this age have cohesion, agreement and stability in their world. The six year old's plethora of questions around these issues may reflect anxiety about differences as well as constructive wishes to try and sort it out in their own mind.

THE SIX YEAR OLD AND THE FACTS OF LIFE

Fantasy and fairy stories

A small child's life is not complete without fantasy and fairy stories which embody and express in so many different ways their internal realities, hopes, fears and disappointments. At this age the world of fantasy is not very far removed from reality, as the child is only just beginning to sort out belief in stories and belief in external reality. The myths of Father Christmas and the Tooth Fairy are fun and many parents feel loth to spoil the illusion. Perhaps these figures represent an ideal father or mother who gives everything the child wants without asking anything in return, in contrast to real parents who cannot gratify all the child's wishes, and who impose rules and limits and so on. Most children by the age of six have a pretty good idea that Father Christmas and the tooth fairy do not actually exist, but go along with the fantasy precisely because it is fun for parents and children. They seem to have a great capacity to believe and not believe in them at the same time. Children at the theatre or at a film become very excited and sometimes frightened because the play becomes confused with reality. One father recalled the sixth birthday party of his son, when he put on a puppet show for the children. The theatre and puppets were toy ones and father could be seen as large as life behind the stage manipulating the puppets, but this in no way distracted the children who watched open-mouthed as the story unfolded and shouted excitedly when the action called for it.

CHAPTER FOUR

THE SIX YEAR OLD AND EVERYDAY LIFE

Mrs Thompson has three children, Elizabeth who is seven and in the top infant class, Charlie, who is just six and Chloë, who is two and a half. When she collects the children from school, Elizabeth comes out skipping along, hair all over the place and so engrossed in conversation with her best friend that she scarcely notices her mother waiting with Chloë in the pushchair. By contrast, Charlie comes running out looking eagerly for her. As soon as he sees her his face changes; he gives a brief scowl in Chloë's direction and begins angry demands for a drink of orange juice which he wants "now". Mrs Thompson explains that she hasn't got orange juice with her but he can have some when they get home. This seems no good for Charlie and he becomes increasingly tearful and furious. Mrs Thompson cannot console him and at first feels upset and guilty at Charlie's distress. He continues to cry and demand orange juice and the episode threatens to turn into a full-scale tantrum. Mrs Thompson begins to be irritated and also feels a little ashamed of her son's angry behaviour. The journey home is fraught and miserable.

This has been going on for just over a week now and Mrs Thompson is at her wits' end to know what to do. She knows that in school Charlie is all right and has grown used to his new male teacher, who assured Mrs Thompson that he is getting on well with the other children and the work, though tending to be a quiet, reserved member of the class. As soon as they are home and they have all had orange juice and a biscuit, Charlie's good humour is restored and he settles comfortably with Elizabeth to watch television. Mrs Thompson, however, continues to feel as though she has been dragged through a hedge backwards by Charlie. She also feels upset that the family reunion at the end of the day, instead of being a pleasure, is becoming tense and difficult for everyone. Half-term is coming up. She has to sort out what to do with the children so that she can get to her job at least some of the time. Charlie is bound to demand yet again that they have the classroom hamster for the week – it really is someone else's turn. Mrs Thompson thinks of her neighbour, Mrs Smith, whose daughter is in the same class as Charlie – but she is having a hard time as her husband has left the family recently and the last thing she needs at the moment is the classroom pet. Mrs Thompson sits drinking her tea and relishing the peace and quiet while the children are watching television. She still feels rather angry with Charlie and does not much feel like agreeing to have the hamster. She decides she will take orange juice and biscuits to school with her tomorrow – maybe that will forestall another outburst.

Most parents of young children will recognise these kind of day-to-day dilemmas that Mrs Thompson was facing. Having children of very different temperaments like Elizabeth and Charlie, while adding to the richness of family life, in itself presents problems of responding to their different needs. When to "give in" to a child, and when to give precedence to their own moods and preferences is an example of the kind of quandaries that parents with young children have to struggle with.

Separation and divorce

In the previous chapters we have been looking at issues concerning the world of the six year old predominantly in the context of a family with two parents. Of course these issues apply to young children generally but it seems important to think about the painful situation which arises when the parents' relationship breaks down as it had with Mrs Thompson's neighbour. Recent surveys show that a quarter of all children experience parental separation before they are 16. There were several children in Charlie's class whose parents had split up. Mrs Thompson remembered a time when her own marriage was going through a bad spell and separation had been on the cards. They had managed to patch things up but she had a good idea of what Mr and Mrs Smith were going through and had often given temporary refuge to their children, Elaine and Tom.

Young children derive much security from being in a family with two parents who are in a relationship which is basically friendly and sexually satisfying to both partners. Parents who are in the main mutually supportive and happy in their marriage will be more able to manage their child's ups and downs, than parents who are very rivalrous and unhappy with each other. Young children feel protected and supported by parents who are a source of strength to each other and this experience helps them as they grow and mature and come to form relationships of their own.

In reality, however, it is not always possible to provide this security. Marriages or partnerships often break down to a point where separation or divorce seems the only answer. Sometimes it may be the best solution for everyone if the situation in the family has become unbearable. Indeed a young child living in an atmosphere of bitter hostility may, like the parents, feel considerable relief when they finally separate. Whether the antagonism is expressed openly in violent rows, or covertly in cold silences, your ordinarily alert six year old will be aware before any actual separation takes place that all is not well between the parents.

Parental separation brings with it profound changes in the lives of children, including changes in the nature of their relationships to each parent. There is usually the effective loss of one parent (usually the father); sometimes the need to move house and very possibly a change in financial circumstances.

Elaine and Tom were aged six and nine when their parents separated. Their father, Mr Smith, left the family home after discovering his wife was having an affair. The relationship had been tense for a while as Mr Smith worked long hours trying to set up in business on his own having been made redundant two years previously. He was often preoccupied and tired when he was at home. Mrs Smith felt increasingly lonely and left to run the house and look after the children on her own. Although Mrs Smith gave up the liaison and wanted to try and rebuild the marriage, Mr Smith felt too hurt and they finally decided to separate. Mr Smith moved into separate accommodation and Mrs Smith stayed in the family home with Elaine and Tom. The divorce was acrimonious as feelings were running high – Mr Smith felt betrayed and humiliated by his wife's infidelity and Mrs Smith felt angry that her attempts to put things right were rebuffed. There were bitter squabbles about arrangements for Mr Smith to see Elaine and Tom, which were complicated by the childrens' reactions to their father's departure. Elaine in particular found it very difficult to come to terms with what was happening. Being younger she could not grasp as clearly as Tom, the complexities of the situation. She was especially close to her father, quite a "Daddy's girl" in fact, but she refused to see him for a long time which caused him great sadness and worry. From Elaine's point of view it may have seemed that her father was wrong to leave and that he had rejected her. She may have also felt disappointed that he couldn't put everything right as fathers are supposed to do. Mrs Smith for her part had to bear the brunt of Elaine's anger and upset and this was especially difficult as she had to manage her own feelings of anger and bitterness about the separation. Tom coped in a different way – he became quiet and withdrawn where Elaine was more open in her rages and tantrums. For a while his schoolwork deteriorated but picked up again as time went by and when the access arrangements were established. He seemed to derive respite also by becoming more involved in his own activities, particularly playing football which he loved.

Divorcing parents sometimes become so embroiled and unhappy in their marital distress that finding the emotional resources to attend to the needs of their children becomes terribly difficult. This may drive them to behave in the child's presence as though nothing is happening, perhaps because they feel guilty and worried about the effects of their actions, and in the belief that by so doing they are sparing the child unhappiness. Mr and Mrs Smith were both devoted to their children but at the time when their feelings towards each other were particularly raw and angry they were acutely aware of the temptation to turn to one or other of the children in a collusive way in order to punish and denigrate the other parent. Small children like Elaine feel frightened and bewildered when their parents separate because their loyalties are very torn. They feel at the mercy of events and they do not yet have the capacity to think about the complexities of their parents' relationship. One of the things that helped Elaine during this unhappy period was that she had a good relationship with Tom and to some extent they could console each other.

If the relationship has broken down to the extent that there is no amicable basis from which to negotiate the children's interests, it may be important to enlist outside help. Many district courts run a mediation service which aims specifically to deal with practical aspects of the children's needs such as settling access arrangements. The local Child Guidance Service or Relate can also offer the opportunity for warring parents to discuss the practical issues with an uninvolved third person. There are several helpful books available to help parents think about the issues involved and one or two of these will be listed at the end of this book.

For a six year old like Elaine the far-reaching implications of the parents' separation can be less readily understood than for her brother Tom. But not all children react like Elaine. Some may attempt to cope with their fears and anxieties by trying to convince themselves and those around them that there is nothing wrong and this may result in a sort of false independence which masks deeper fears. At such a stressful time the parents may be tempted to go along with this in order to keep the peace. Elaine's reactions to her parents separation were, in a way, straightforward in that she seemed to know what she was angry about and could express it openly. Some six year olds find this difficult and will rather express their feelings in other ways.

Because children at this age are still very dependent on their parents they feel frightened about what will happen to them – it will relieve some of the uncertainty if the parents can acknowledge openly that they are no longer getting on well enough to live together. If a parent has left the home it is very important not to hedge or fob the child off with a story like "Daddy has gone on holiday for a little while." Being truthful in a simple way will go a long way to reassuring young children that they are being taken seriously and that their welfare and feelings are not forgotten.

Whatever the circumstances of the separation, there is no getting away from the painful fact that it is bound to cause some upset and disturbance – indeed a child who appeared not to be affected in any way would be much more of a cause for worry. Letting the child's teacher know that there are problems at home will enable her to approach possible disturbances in the child's behaviour or learning in school with more understanding.

Small children almost always feel that it is somehow their fault if their parents' marriage breaks down and they will need much reassurance about this. They also need to know that both their parents are at least still united in loving them and can, to some extent work, together for their welfare. Knowing too, that loving one parent does not mean hating the other will help a young child with divided loyalties; and in this regard it is terribly important to resist the temptation, as Mrs Smith managed to do, to turn the child against the other parent.

Bringing things home from school

For the most part in this book we have been talking about the early experiences our six year olds take with them into the wider world of school and friends. But now the fruits of their labours, experiences and observations are brought back into the family for further appraisal and consideration. In practical terms this may mean that your kitchen walls, cupboards, and fridge door are festooned with colourful drawings and paintings. The window ledge or sideboard may be home to glorious constructions of cardboard, cereal packets and toilet rolls, stuck with tissue paper or macaroni and held together with oceans of glue. Your ornamental pots may be full of marbles and wrinkled conkers – abandoned remnants of former games and crazes. The gaudy Christmas or Easter card painstakingly put together by an eager six year old is infinitely more gratifying to a proud parent than a shop-bought card. The latest craze in words will roll around the house like the discarded marbles – everything is "ace" or "fab" or "rubbish", and recently heard lavatorial jokes will be giggled about.

We saw, too, how Charlie brought home to his mother his tired grumpiness, as though he had just about managed to cope with his day at school, and then seemed to need to let all the frustrations and strains fall into his mother's lap. The family, especially mother, provides a vital place where the stresses of the day can be accommodated in a particular and familiar way.

Mrs Jenkins recalled how her daughter Mandy had been having a difficult time with a friend in her class who had gone off with another group, leaving Mandy out. At supper one day Mandy declared she wasn't going to be friends with her any more and she was clearly quite upset. Mr Jenkins, by way of sympathy, talked about a supervisor at work whom he didn't like very much and Mrs Jenkins joined in with some difficulties she had with a colleague at her work. The family then started to imagine a ghastly dinner party to which all these problematic people would be invited and to laugh as the children thought of horrible food to dish up to them. By the end of the meal Mandy was more cheerful, feeling perhaps that she was not alone in having to cope with such problems and that her family could understand how she felt.

Young children in these early years at school are making

friends and learning that families behave in very different ways from their own. When they go to play in a friend's house they will sense a different atmosphere and observe the kind of manners and expectations other parents have of their children. Charlie, the little boy mentioned above, had made friends with an Asian boy in his class and went one day after school to play. When he came home he was rather quiet and finally told his mother that he didn't want to go to Ali's again and when pressed to say why, he said it was because "his house smelt funny". Mrs Thompson was relieved that it was nothing more serious, and explained to Charlie about spices and curries – one day they might take him out for a curry. Charlie was also surprised at the idea that Ali might have the same reaction when he came to Charlie's house.

Your six year old will bring home many new experiences like Charlie and will begin to make comparisons and question why things are done as they are in his family. One of the most common areas where parents are put into a quandary is when your child wants something his other friends at school have got. If this amounts to packets of marbles for instance, it is not so bad but today it is as likely to be expensive toys like computer games or a complete stately home set for a Cindy doll! For most parents financial circumstances will help decide the issue, but there may also be other less clearly defined reasons for saying "no" or making the child wait for Christmas or birthday. Perhaps just a vague feeling that "it isn't right" or that "it wouldn't be good for the child". Katy, aged seven, was putting enormous pressure on her parents to let her have a television in her room and countered her parents refusal with "well Mary's parents let her have one". This is a tricky situation that crops up time and time again in various ways now that your youngster is out and about. Mary's parents are being paraded as the really "good" parents while Katy's parents are the "meanies". The dilemma is whether to try and "keep up with the Jones's" or stick to your guns about how you want to do things. Over this issue Katy's parents continued to say "no" to Katy who complained bitterly for several days that "it wasn't fair – and anyway they had a television in their bedroom, so why couldn't she?"

Of course, sometimes children have a point when they challenge some rule or prohibition imposed by their parents. Parents then are obliged to reconsider their strictures and work out whether they are being unreasonable or arbitrary.

A. A. Milne's son, the original Christopher Robin, described an amusing incident in his biography of his father, when the latter was trying to get his young son to be polite at the table. The child was told not to sit holding his knife and fork pointing upwards between mouthfuls. He asked his father, "why not?" and A. A. Milne, who was not, by all accounts, a strict disciplinarian, did not know how to answer this perfectly reasonable question. Finally he resorted to humour; he replied "Well, someone might come crashing through the ceiling and land on your fork and that wouldn't be very nice."

Television and computer games

Apart from financial reasons, Katy's parents were unwilling to allow her a television in her bedroom because they were worried she would become addicted to it and never do anything else. The same kind of concern also extends to computer games. This is a real worry for most parents as television and computers now play such a huge role in our lives. Before the age of six children seem not to be particularly interested except for short periods, as their attention span is limited. But by six the television bug tends to strike and children may become more inclined to sit and watch almost anything. We saw how Charlie and Elizabeth collapsed in front of the television when they got home from school. Like adults, children need some time to relax after a tiring day at school and watching television gives them a chance to unwind. The trouble starts when they seem reluctant to do anything else, or when they go from the television to playing computer games. There is no doubt that television can be a great boon to a busy or tired mother when there is a need to have children quietly occupied. It is sometimes however, very tempting to let children sit for long periods watching television or playing computer games and this can prevent more sociable activities developing, and this is where the danger of young children becoming addicted begins. Children whose parents are willing to encourage and take part in their activities and games, and can be a bit firm about how much telvision they watch, are less likely to become addicted.

It is also not only how much television their small children are watching but what they watch that often worries parents, as more explicitly violent or sexual scenes are shown. Katy's parents felt that by allowing Katy a television in her bedroom she would not only be tempted to watch alone rather than be with the family, but they would have less control over what she was watching, possibly late at night.

There are many vexed questions around this to which there seems to be no right answer. Should small children watch scenes of terrible famine in the news? Is there any harm in them watching cops and robbers films where shooting people is commonplace and even sometimes shown as the right thing to do? Are these films any worse than cowboys and Indians which seem to be more accepted? Does it matter if children see scenes of sexual intercourse?

There is undoubtedly an extreme kind of cruel violence or sexuality which is too strong for young children to cope with and from which they need to be protected. Yet there is a huge area where it is not so clear. The cartoon Tom and Jerry is extremely violent. Many children love it and seem oblivious to the violence while others cannot watch it. The classic film Bambi reduces most children, and often their parents too, to tears yet for some small children it is too frightening to watch. This does seem to come back to the point that children differ a great deal in what frightens and upsets them. That Tom and Jerry and Bambi are cartoons and therefore clearly not "real" does not seem to make much difference for children at this age. It seems likely that upsetting events and scenes touch on different raw feelings in individual children. Many parents of six year olds know that sleeplessness or nightmares can follow a frightening television programme or video. This may happen when a child has some inner fears and worries, especially about the extent and unruliness or his own anger, which are stirred up by the vividness of the scenes.

THE SIX YEAR OLD AND EVERYDAY LIFE

Discipline

The need for discipline from parents changes as six year olds develop their own sense of what is right or acceptable and become more able to control their destructive or anti-social impulses. Quite small children are quick to pick up and remember the boundaries imposed on them by their parents – this can be seen when a crawling infant goes to an electric plug and looks back at mother, clearly with the awareness that it is something he has been told not to touch. A child at that age however, still needs a parent to step in to reinforce the control and discipline. A three year old will have a more sophisticated idea of what is permissible. The Winton family were having a family Christmas together with cousins, so there were many children in the house. A cousin, Sam, aged seven, had been given a pound note as one of his presents and it had gone missing. Crisis! "Has anyone seen Sam's pound note?" all the children were asked. When it came to Rachel who was three, she shook her head vigorously, but then added rather anxiously "and it's not in my toy till!" The pound was restored to Sam and calm returned. It would be too strong to say that Rachel had "stolen" Sam's pound note but she was already showing the beginnings of what we would call an inner conscience about what she had done. This developing conscience, derived from the parents' firmness in the early years will help Rachel to exercise gradually her own self-control. The six year old, who in general has had an experience of firmness when it is necessary, combined with a reasonable amount of freedom to express her own wishes and have them taken seriously, will be greatly helped to feel "at home" in the more disciplined world of school.

FURTHER READING

Thinking about Infants and Young Children, Martha Harris, Cluny Press, Perthshire, 1983
Divorce and Your Children, Anne Hooper; Robson Books, London, 1990
Surviving the Breakup, Judith Wallerstein and Joan Berlin Kelly, Grant McIntyre, 1980
The Role of the School in the Libidinal Development of the Child, Melanie Klein, in "1921–45 Contributions to Psychoanalysis", Hogarth Press, London, 1948

HELPFUL ORGANISATIONS

Educational Psychology Services (see Local Education Authority)
Child and Family Services (see Local Health Authority)
Cruse - Bereavement Care and Counselling, Sheen Rd. Richmond, London. (Tel 081 940 4818)
Family Mediators Association; 7 Raeburn Close, London NW11. (Tel 081 458 3166)
Relate Marriage Guidance, Little Church Street, Rugby. (Tel 0788 573241)

UNDERSTANDING YOUR CHILD

ORDER FORM FOR TITLES IN THIS SERIES

Send to: Rosendale Press Ltd., Premier House
10 Greycoat Place, London SW1P 1SB

Price per volume: £4.75 inc. post & packing

Understanding Your Baby by Lisa Miller	. . . . . copies
Understanding Your 1 Year Old by Deborah Steiner	. . . . . copies
Understanding Your 2 Year Old by Susan Reid	. . . . . copies
Understanding Your 3 Year Old by Judith Trowell	. . . . . copies
Understanding Your 4 Year Old by Lisa Miller	. . . . . copies
Understanding Your 5 Year Old by Lesley Holditch	. . . . . copies

Price per volume: £5.65 inc. post & packing

Understanding Your 6 Year Old by Deborah Steiner	. . . . . copies
Understanding Your 7 Year Old by Elsie Osborne	. . . . . copies
Understanding Your 8 Year Old by Lisa Miller	. . . . . copies
Understanding Your 9 Year Old by Dora Lush	. . . . . copies
Understanding Your 10 Year Old by Jonathan Bradley	. . . . . copies
Understanding Your 11 Year Old by Eileen Orford	. . . . . copies
Understanding Your Handicapped Child by Valerie Sinason	. . . . copies

Total amount enclosed: £. . . . .
Name . . . .
Address . . . .
. . . . Post code . . . .